AN
ALBUM OF
WORLD WAR I

AN
ALBUM
OF
WORLD WAR I
BY DOROTHY AND THOMAS HOOBLER

FRANKLIN WATTS | NEW YORK | LONDON | 1976

Cover design by Nick Krenitsky

Photographs courtesy of: American Expedition
Forces (National Archives): p. 77 (top); Army
News Features: p. 70; Bettman Archives: p. 6
(top); Bilderdienst Suddeutscher Verlag: p. 16;
French Embassy Press & Information Division: pp.
13, 19 (top), 30, 49 (bottom), 57, 71, 73 (left);
Imperial War Museum: pp. 9, 23 (top), 32, 35,
41, 45, 56 (left), 62, 84 (bottom); International
Red Cross Committee: pp. 47, 65 (bottom); Library of Congress: 17, 19 (bottom), 20 (top), 25,
34 (bottom), 37 (top), 38 (bottom), 53 (right),
65 (top), 76; National Archives: pp. 33, 44; New
York Public Library: p. 56 (right); New York
State Historical Society: p. 75; Novosti (Sovfoto):
pp. 50, 77; Osterreichische Nationalbibliotheil: pp.
14 (top), 40; Radio Times Hulton Picture Library:
pp. 31, 37 (bottom), 46, 66, 74, 87 (top); Soviet
Life (Sovfoto): p. 93; Sovfoto: p. 6 (bottom);
Tass (Sovfoto): p. 61 (right); United Press International: p. 14 (bottom); U.S. Army: p. 87 (bottom); U.S. Signal Corps (National Archives): pp.
11, 12, 20 (bottom), 21, 23 (bottom), 24 (bottom), 34 (top), 36, 42, 49 (top), 52, 53 (left),
54, 58, 68, 77 (left), 78 (left), 82, 83, 84 (top),
88 (top); U.S. War Department General Staff
(National Archives): pp. 7, 10, 24 (top), 27, 28,
29, 38 (top and middle), 39, 43, 48, 51, 54, 55,
59, 61 (left), 63, 64, 67, 69, 73 (right), 78
(right), 81, 88 (bottom), 90, 91.

Library of Congress Cataloging in Publication Data

Hoobler, Dorothy.
  An album of World War I.

  Includes index.
  SUMMARY: An account of World War I including its causes, campaigns and battles, outcome,
peace treaty, and effects.
  1. European War, 1914–1918 — Juvenile lit-
erature. [1. European War, 1914–1918] I. Hoobler,
Thomas, joint author. II. Title.
D522.7.H66   940.3   75–44281
ISBN 0–531–01169–0

⚜ CONTENTS ⚜

PROLOGUE

Above: a pleasant British garden party shows the way the upper classes in Europe lived before the war. Below: a women's demonstration in Russia in 1905.

EUROPE BEFORE THE WAR

In 1914 the countries of Europe were the wealthiest and most powerful the world had ever known. Europeans controlled much of the world's manufacturing, mining, and trade.

On the surface, European life was glittering and gay — at least for the wealthy. Expensive homes, lively cafés, and beautiful country scenes made European life look gloriously happy.

Underneath the surface, there was some unrest. Many European workers and farmers did not share in Europe's wealth. Strikes, protests, assassinations, and riots showed their discontent.

But the majority were confident about the future. They thought more progress would allow all Europeans to share in the prosperity.

EUROPE AFTER THE WAR

By 1918 Europe was devastated. Eight and a half millon soldiers were dead. Many more were wounded or missing. Much of Europe's wealth had been spent on the war. Bitterness replaced the old confidence in the future. Governments had fallen; the map of Europe had changed forever.

"The war to end all wars," as World War I was called, only planted the seeds for a new and more terrible war. Only thirty-one years later, World War II broke out and tore Europe apart again.

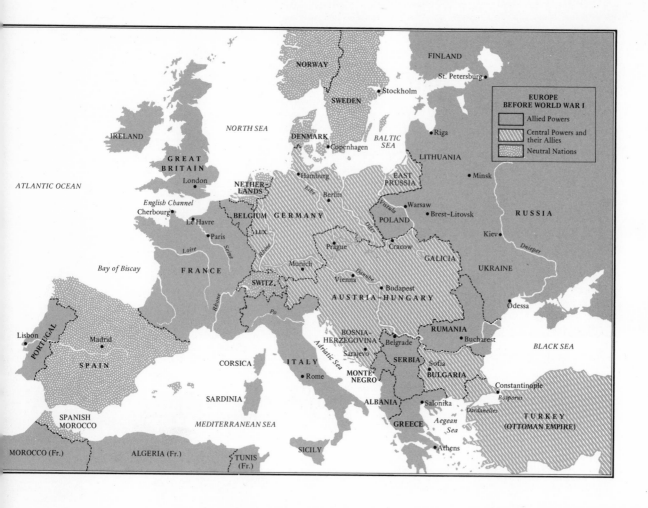

THE CAUSES OF THE WAR

The war that would destroy European society had been coming for a long time. The nineteenth century had been an era of great progress, and of turmoil and conflict as well. New nations had been created. The balance of power that existed in 1815, at the end of the era of Napoleon, was disturbed.

Adding to the danger was a false sense of security. Local wars had flared up in the nineteenth century, but a major war was regarded as unlikely. Looking back at 1914 today, however, we can see that each of the major countries of Europe had interests that would bring it into conflict with at least one of the other great powers.

The Major Combatants

- The GERMAN EMPIRE had been created in 1871. Included in its territory were the provinces of Alsace and Lorraine, taken from France. Now Germany was the leading power on the Continent. But Germany was not secure. Directly to the west was France, waiting for the chance to reclaim Alsace-Lorraine. To the east was Russia, recently allied with France. And on the seas the rapidly growing German navy competed with the more powerful British navy.

- FRANCE had not forgotten its humiliating defeat at the hands of Germany in 1871. France was waiting for the chance to reestablish its power on the Continent. France was willing to ally itself with another longtime enemy, Britain, to strengthen its hand against Germany.

- The AUSTRO-HUNGARIAN EMPIRE was not a nation of one people, but an empire of many nationalities. The peoples that made up the empire were mainly Austrians, Hungarians, and Slavs. But the Austrians and Hungarians ruled the empire. Many Slavs who lived in the provinces of Bosnia and Herzegovina wanted to be part of the new nation of Serbia. Furthermore, Rumania and Italy had designs on territory within the empire. Russian ambitions in the Balkans brought them into conflict with the Austro-Hungarians.

- ITALY had become a nation in 1870. But it wanted more territory, some of which belonged to the Austro-Hungarian Empire. Italy also wanted colonies in North Africa, which conflicted with French aims.

- GREAT BRITAIN had traditionally followed a policy of neutrality, which served it well. Yet some Britons were now calling for new alliances, to counter the rising power of the German Empire. Britain depended on industrial strength for survival. Germany was a threat to that strength, as well as to Britain's naval power.

Kaiser Wilhelm II of Germany (left) and Emperor Franz Joseph of Austria-Hungary were allies. Wilhelm backed Franz Joseph's efforts to keep his empire together.

Raymond Poincaré (left) was president of France.
George V (right) was king of England.
They are shown here with their wives.
Britain and France, often enemies in the past,
were starting to see each other as allies.

- RUSSIA had been defeated by the Japanese in 1905 and was troubled by unrest within its borders. Russia felt a need to prove its strength to the other nations of Europe. It also desired to extend its influence and protection over the Slavs in Balkan countries.

- The OTTOMAN EMPIRE (the empire of Turkey) was known as the "sick man of Europe." The new nations in the Balkans — Serbia, Bulgaria, Rumania, and Greece — had broken off from the empire. The nations of Europe feared the Ottoman Empire would collapse and there would be a fight for its territory. Russia, in particular, wanted the Dardanelles Strait, a strategic part of the empire.

- SERBIA had become a nation during the nineteenth century. But it was not satisfied with its territory. It wanted the South Slavic territories in the Austro-Hungarian Empire. It also gave some assistance to the Serbian nationalists within Austria-Hungary — one of whom would fire the shot that ignited World War I.

Sources of Friction between the Powers

- In addition to these political conflicts, the causes of the war included such forces as NATIONALISM, or patriotism. Nationalism led

European nations to compete for the largest army and navy, or the greatest industrial development. It also gave groups of subject peoples the idea of forming independent nations of their own.

● MILITARISM, another cause of the war, was similar to the arms race of today. Because Britain had a great navy, Germany wanted a great navy too. Germany and France competed for larger armies. The more one nation built up its army and navy, the more other nations felt they had to do the same.

● Another cause was that European nations ruled smaller countries, called colonies, and competed with each other to amass more colonies. Gathering colonies became known as IMPERIALISM. Both France and Britain had many colonies in Africa and Asia. Now Germany and Italy decided they wanted a colonial empire too.

● Finally, there was the SYSTEM OF ALLIANCES. For twenty years, the nations of Europe had been making alliances. It was thought the alliances would promote peace. Each country would be protected by others in case of war, making it foolish for one country to wage war on another.

The danger of these alliances was that an argument between two countries could draw all the other nations into the fight. This is just what happened when a conflict between Austria-Hungary and Serbia led to World War I.

In the summer of 1914 there were two alliances. *The Triple Alliance*, composed of Germany, Austria-Hungary, and Italy, stood opposed to the *Triple Entente*, composed of Britain, France, and Russia.

The Czar (emperor) of Russia, Nicholas II, is seen here reviewing his troops. Russia allied itself with Britain and France because of its growing rivalry with Austria-Hungary in the Balkans and a fear of Germany.

WAR PLANS

The Schlieffen Plan

The nations of Europe had prepared secret war plans. As early as 1905 a German general named Schlieffen designed a plan that became the basis for German strategy in 1914.

Schlieffen realized that since France and Russia were allies, Germany would have to fight both of them — Russia to the east, and France to the west.

Schlieffen expected the Russians to take a long time to bring their army into battle, because the Russian army was poorly trained and equipped. So he planned to concentrate the German forces in the west in order to defeat France quickly. Then Germany could turn its full force on the Russians.

Schlieffen knew that a *direct attack* on France would take too long. So he planned to have a small force engage the French at the French-German border and allow itself to be pushed back slowly into Germany. Meanwhile, the greater part of the German forces would march through the neutral country of Belgium. They would cross into France and

*General **Helmuth von Moltke** was the German army chief of staff in 1914. He was trained in the Schlieffen Plan but modified it when the Germans began the war.*

General Joffre (left) was leader of the French army at the beginning of the war. Impressed by the leadership of General Ferdinand Foch (right), Joffre appointed him his assistant. By the end of the war, Foch was commander of all the troops on the western front.

swing around to trap the French army fighting at the French-German border.

The Germans were aware that an invasion of Belgium would bring other countries into the war, particularly Britain. But they felt that a quick victory was worth the risk.

When war did break out, von Moltke, now the German commander, changed the Schlieffen plan slightly. He concentrated more forces at the German-French border than Schlieffen had intended. The result was that the stronger German forces pushed the French back to a position where they could defend themselves better against the Germans coming from Belgium.

The French Plan

The French were dedicated to taking back Alsace-Lorraine, on the other side of the French-German border. Therefore the French plan was to attack in force directly at the border.

The French were also counting on the fighting spirit of their army. They felt that Alsace-Lorraine was something every Frenchman would fight for with enthusiasm.

Unfortunately, the war would last much longer than either side expected. The patriotic appeals would become a horrible joke in the face of millions of deaths.

1914

ASSASSINATION AND
THE ROAD TO WAR

● On JUNE 28, 1914, Gavrilo Princip, a nineteen-year-old Serbian revolutionary, fired two pistol shots. One killed Archduke Franz Ferdinand, the nephew of Emperor Franz Joseph of Austria-Hungary and heir to the Austrian throne. The other killed Sophie, his wife.

● Austria-Hungary held Serbia responsible. On JULY 5 Austria asked for and received from Germany a "blank check" of support for any action Austria-Hungary might take against Serbia.

● On JULY 23 Austria sent a series of demands to the Serbians. The demands were designed to humiliate and virtually destroy the Serbian nation. Still, Serbia agreed to most *but not all* of the demands.

● Austria reacted on JULY 28 by declaring war on Serbia. The Russians prepared to defend Serbia. On JULY 31 the Germans sent a warning to Russia to stop mobilizing its army for war. The Russians ignored the warning, and Germany declared war on Russia on AUGUST 1. France came to the aid of its Russian ally by declaring war on Germany. The British hesitated, but when the Germans marched into Belgium, they declared war on Germany on AUGUST 4.

Italy, the third member of the Triple Alliance, refused to back Germany and Austria-Hungary. Italy claimed the Triple Alliance was for defensive purposes only and Austria's declaration of war against Serbia was not defensive.

So in August, 1914, the guns of war went off. The system of alliances for keeping peace had brought the great nations of Europe into war with one another.

*Above: Archduke **Franz Ferdinand** and his wife, **Sophie**, moments before they were shot. Sophie has an umbrella to protect her from the sun. Their car made a wrong turn, and when it stopped to back up, **Gavrilo Princip** rushed from the crowd with a pistol. Below: police and soldiers take Princip (second from right) to prison after the assassination.*

A crowd in Berlin cheers the German soldiers marching off to war. The soldiers are carrying flowers in their rifles, and a civilian has taken a helmet and jumped into line.

ACTION IN THE WEST

The German Attack on Belgium

On August 4 waves of gray-coated German soldiers marched confidently into Belgium. The Kaiser had told his soldiers they would be home before the leaves fell. They expected little resistance.

King Albert of Belgium prepared to put up a stiff fight, telling his men to "hold to the end." A key to the Belgian defense was the city of Liège, which was protected by a circle of forts. It stood directly in the path of the oncoming Germans.

Sixty thousand Germans attacked Liège, which was defended by only 25,000 Belgians. At first the Belgians held. But a little-known German commander named Ludendorff led a brigade of soldiers between the defending forts and captured the city. German artillery soon arrived and destroyed the remaining defenses.

The Germans drove on. By August 20 they had captured Brussels, the capital of Belgium. The Germans shot Belgian civilians who resisted the invasion. Later the Allies (as the Triple Entente countries were called) would use these "atrocities" as a propaganda weapon against the Germans.

The successes in Belgium led General von Moltke, the German commander in chief, to transfer some troops to the eastern front, where the Russians had attacked sooner than expected. This move had serious consequences later.

The German March into France

By the end of August the German army had crossed the northern border from Belgium into France. The French had been pushed back from Alsace and Lorraine. The British had landed a small group of soldiers to help the French defend their border.

The British Expeditionary Force, as it was called, was no match for the greater numbers of Germans. The British and French generals decided to fall back to a position they could defend more easily. They retreated to the Marne River.

German troops crossing the border into France from Belgium.

The Battle of the Marne

As the French and British fell back to the Marne, the Germans marched confidently through France. The French government, fearing capture, left Paris. The citizens of Paris panicked. But General Gallieni remained in the city with a small number of French soldiers and organized the citizens for its defense.

The rapid advance had disorganized the German army. Divisions were becoming separated, and communications were not good. When von Moltke gave the order for the German First Army Group to turn east before reaching Paris, the flank (side) of this German army was exposed to Gallieni's forces. General Joffre, the commander in chief of the French army, took advantage of the opportunity.

On September 4, the French attacked the German flank. This was the start of a crucial battle. If the Germans reorganized successfully, they could win a final victory over the French and the British Expeditionary Force.

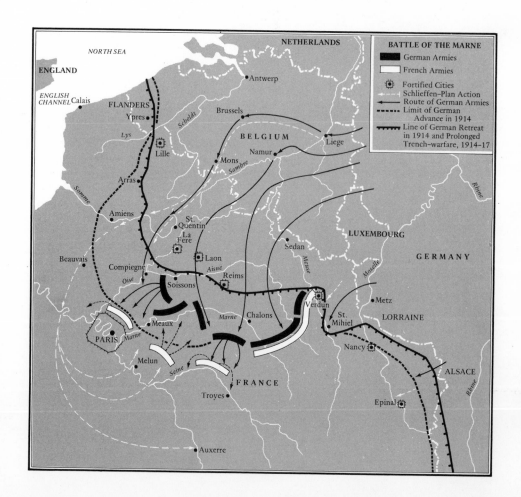

French troops marching north to meet the German advance outside Paris. The taxicabs shown are like the ones later used to transport troops to the battle.

A French general speaks to his troops before battle. The French placed a high value on enthusiasm. Speeches like this were meant to raise the morale of the men.

As the battle raged just north of Paris, General Gallieni realized that reinforcements were needed quickly. What happened next is called the "miracle of the Marne." The horse-drawn taxicabs of Paris were used to drive the French soldiers from Paris to the battle at the Marne River. About 700 taxis were used in two trips to transport all the troops. With the additional men, the French turned back the German drive. By September 11 the Germans were in retreat. They fell back to the Aisne River. France had been saved.

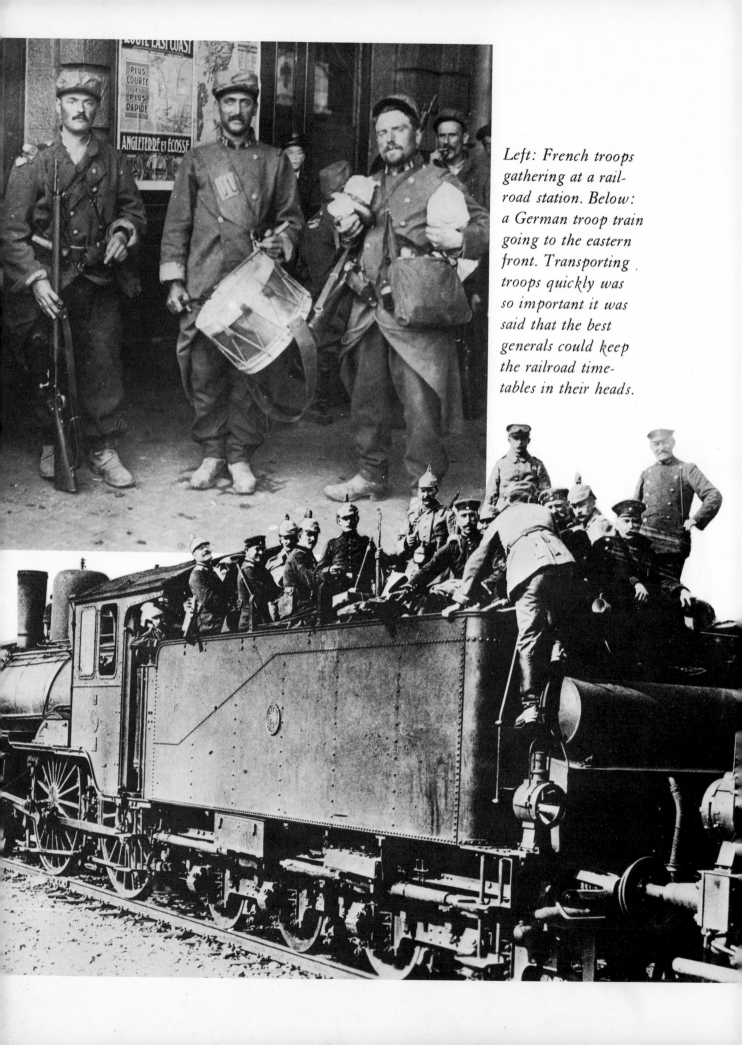

Left: French troops gathering at a railroad station. Below: a German troop train going to the eastern front. Transporting troops quickly was so important it was said that the best generals could keep the railroad timetables in their heads.

The Race to the Sea

After the German retreat, General von Moltke was replaced by General Erich von Falkenhayn as commander of the German army. Then the "race to the sea" began, as the Germans tried to repair von Moltke's blunder of turning east before reaching Paris.

The Germans marched north and west to try to envelop the French flank. The French and British extended their lines to the northwest to keep the Germans from enveloping them. The situation was like an "end run" in football with the sea as the out-of-bounds line. The French and British reached the sea first and blocked the German sweep. But the race did not result in victory for the French and British. Instead, it established a line of opposing troops 400 miles long, from Switzerland to the North Sea.

The First Battle of Ypres

With the two operating forces facing each other, the only battle tactic possible was a frontal attack. The favorite places to attack were bulges in the enemy lines, called "salients." These were hard to defend because they could be attacked from the front and both sides at once.

On October 20 the Germans attacked a salient at the Belgian city of Ypres, a valuable communications and shipping center. The Ypres region was to be the site of four bloody battles during the war. About 250,000 men were killed or wounded at the first battle of Ypres. No ground was gained by either side. This was to be the ghastly pattern of battle on the western front for nearly the entire war.

A German sentry overlooks the English Channel from Belgium. Although the Germans occupied most of Belgium, the Belgian army linked up with the French and British on the North Sea and continued to fight for the rest of the war.

ACTION IN THE EAST

The Battle of Tannenberg

The Russians had promised their French allies that they would attack Germany in East Prussia as soon as war broke out. And, indeed, the Russians moved faster than the Germans expected.

Two Russian armies, one in the north and the other farther south, moved to the East Prussian border. The first army crossed the border on August 21. Outnumbering the German forces in the area by two to one, the Russians broke through the German defense.

The Kaiser brought in General von Hindenburg and General Ludendorff to lead the German forces in East Prussia. The plan was to attack the two branches of the Russian army one at a time.

The southern Russian army was led by General Samsonov. Ludendorff let him advance into Prussia, then attacked at the end of August. The result was a smashing victory for the Germans, known as the Battle of Tannenberg.

The Battle of Masurian Lakes

Two weeks later the Germans turned north and defeated the northern branch of the Russian armies at the Battle of Masurian Lakes. Again Russian casualties were very high. Russia lost about a quarter of a million men in the two battles, and an equal number of Russian prisoners were captured.

Despite their losses, the Russians succeeded in drawing German forces away from the battles in France. This helped the Allied troops at the Marne and saved France.

Right: a company of Russian machine gunners. The Germans knew the Russians' battle plans before Tannenberg because the Russians did not use a code when sending radio messages.

Hopeful and confident, these Russian soldiers rushed into battle. They were inadequately trained and badly led.

Above: this is a Serbian ammunition wagon train near Belgrade during the fighting. Despite their lack of equipment, the Serbs defeated the Austrians. Far right: Montenegrin prisoners of war held by Austria-Hungary. Montenegro was one of the South Slav countries fighting with Serbia. After the war these countries united to form Yugoslavia. Right: this is an Austrian artillery team using a field gun against the Serbs.

The Austrian Offensive

The problems of the Austro-Hungarian Empire were reflected in its army. There was mutual distrust between officers and men. The officers spoke German, and the soldiers spoke Slavic languages. The loyalty of the troops to the empire was often in doubt.

On August 12 Austria-Hungary invaded the tiny country of Serbia. The Austrians were confident of a quick victory, but the Serbians threw them back. By December, 1914, Austria regrouped its army and attacked Serbia again. This time the Austrians managed to capture the Serbian capital of Belgrade. But they could hold it for only four days. The Serbians counterattacked, regained the capital, and forced the Austrians back across the border.

Austria vs. Russia

The Austrians had no more success against the Russians. The Carpathian Mountains formed a natural defense line between Austria-Hungary and the Russian province of Poland. But rather than take a defensive position, the Austrians gambled on an attack. By August 25 Austrian soldiers were deep into Russian Poland. Then the Russians counterattacked and drove the Austrians back to the Carpathian Mountains. The Germans had to send reinforcements to keep the Russian army from advancing farther.

WORLD WAR I
EASTERN AND
WESTERN FRONTS

Neutral Nations
Allied Powers
Central Powers
and their Allies
Eastern Front, 1914
Line of Prolonged
Trench-Warfare
Armistice-Line,
Eastern Front, 1917

THE TWO SIDES
AT THE END OF 1914

At the end of 1914 the opposing armies were digging into trenches all along the eastern and western fronts. Throughout the war these positions would be strengthened. In the east the opposing forces formed a line 1,900 miles long; in the west the line ran from the Alps to the Atlantic.

Advantages and
Disadvantages of Each Side

Germany and Austria-Hungary were called the Central Powers because of their position in the center of Europe. Because these two countries adjoined each other, communications problems were not so great as those of the Allies. Germany was the leader of the Central Powers and made all the war decisions. Finally, Germany controlled Belgium and important French territory that contained 80 percent of France's coal and iron resources.

The Allied side had strengths too. (1) The British navy cut off shipping to the Central Powers. (2) The Allies had the populations of their colonies and Britain's empire to draw on for troops. (3) Russia was showing unexpected strength. The Germans now had to fight the two-front war they had wanted to avoid.

In the long run, the Allies' most important advantage was the sympathy of much of the world because of Germany's actions in Belgium. Both sides needed supplies and help from the United States. World sympathy and British sea power kept this support from going to the Germans.

This is a German observation tower along the trench lines near Ypres. A roof from an old house has been added to camouflage the tower.

1915

Life went on, even though conditions were desperate at Gallipoli. Here a British soldier pours his early-morning tea on the beach. Below: Naval guns landed on the beach at Gallipoli. They were immediately covered with soldiers' overcoats to hide them from view. When the British withdrew, they bombarded the supplies left behind so the Turks could not capture them.

GALLIPOLI

When the Ottoman Empire entered the war on the side of the Central Powers in 1914, it closed off the Dardanelles and Bosporus straits. These straits were important because all shipping to Russia from the Mediterranean had to go through them. Since the northern supply routes to Russia were cut off by the Germans, Russia could no longer receive supplies. The Russians asked for British help in opening the straits.

On February 19, 1915, British ships bombarded the Turkish forts along the straits and attempted to steam through. The Turks, however, had mined the straits, and the British had to turn back.

Next the British tried a land invasion. Using Australian and New Zealand soldiers (called ANZACS), the British landed at several beaches on the Gallipoli Peninsula. But the beaches were overlooked by steep hills, at the top of which the Turks had placed batteries of machine guns. Despite great efforts, the Anzacs were not able to scale the hills and take Gallipoli.

In December the British decided to withdraw. They had lost over 200,000 men, and in the retreat they feared losing many more. But General Charles Monro managed to evacuate the remaining 200,000 men in the middle of the night without losing a single one. The Turks didn't even know the British had gone. For several hours they continued to fire at the empty British positions.

Austrlian soldiers attacking a Turkish position. One of the landing beaches was called Anzac Cove, after the initials of the Australian and New Zealand Army Corps.

ACTION IN THE WEST

The Battle of Neuve Chapelle

In trench warfare the defense had an advantage over the offense. But before the generals realized this, they threw away hundreds of thousands of lives trying to break through enemy lines. Only a few yards of territory changed hands in the bloody trench attacks.

The first of these attacks was on March 10. The British bombarded a 2,000-yard-long front at Neuve Chapelle for 35 minutes. Because the Germans were surprised, the British at first broke through their lines. Then the Germans regrouped and pushed the British back.

Below: camouflage was an important part of trench fortification. This field gun could be fired with the tree branches attached. The ramp behind the wheels helped to absorb the recoil when the gun fired. Afterward, it would roll back into position. The opposing lines set up barriers in front of their trenches to make attacks more difficult. At left is a trap set up to trip attacking soldiers.

German soldiers, protected by gas masks, advancing through a cloud of gas. The Germans thought the advantage of gas would be to hide attacking troops. They didn't realize the other side would panic and run.

The Second Battle of Ypres

The Germans still wanted to break through the salient at the town of Ypres. They decided to use a new secret weapon — gas. German deserters and prisoners told the British and French of these plans but the Allied generals did nothing about this information.

On April 22 a greenish cloud floated toward the Allied lines. French colonial troops from North Africa were the first to feel its effects. The gas was chlorine, and it burned the inside of the soldiers' throats and noses so that many choked to death. The Allied soldiers fled, and the French line was broken.

Suddenly there was a 4½-mile gap in the Allied lines. But the Germans hadn't assembled enough men to take advantage of the effect of the gas. By the time the Germans were able to attack effectively, the Allies had sent up more men to block their path.

After the first gas attack, the Germans lost the advantage of surprise. The Allied soldiers protected themselves by wrapping wet bandages across their faces. Soon the Allied side developed gas of its own, and gas masks became part of the standard equipment of both sides.

The Allied Offensive in Champagne

General Joffre still believed the war could be won by a frontal assault on the enemy lines. He ordered a number of attacks in the area of Champagne in September, 1915. At the same time, the British attacked the German lines farther north in Artois.

After a long bombardment, the German line was pierced in both places, but the territory gained by the Allies was slight. Yet the price was high. The Allies lost 242,000 soldiers, and the Germans 141,000.

Left: in between the opposing lines of trenches the soldiers placed barbed wire and land mines to slow down an enemy attack. Attacking troops caught by such traps could be cut down by machine-gun fire from the trenches. For this reason, the area between the trenches came to be called "no-man's-land." Above: German soldiers are digging out a railroad tunnel blown up by Belgians. Cutting the railroad lines could slow down enemy troop movements and give the other side time to prepare a defense.

Right: German troops advancing toward Warsaw, Poland, which they took in early August. Hindenburg and Ludendorff demanded more troops from the command in the west in the hope they could completely destroy the Russian army. Below: Russian prisoners in Poland. By the end of 1915 more than 2 million Russians had been taken prisoner, and another 2 million Russians had been killed or wounded.

ACTION IN THE EAST

The Battle for Poland

The battles of 1914 showed that the Russians could defeat the Austrians but not the Germans. With their supply lines cut off at the Dardanelles, the Russians ran low on weapons and ammunition. Some Russian soldiers went into battle without any weapons. A Russian army saying was: "We have one good weapon — the living heart of the soldier."

Early in 1915, Grand Duke Nicholas of Russia led a major offensive against the Austrian army at the Carpathian Mountains. But the Germans came to the aid of their Austrian allies. Then the Germans counterattacked against the Russians on May 14. The Russian army broke and fled. The Germans pursued the Russians through most of Poland, captured almost 750,000 Russian prisoners, and took most of Russian Poland.

Even so, the victory was not as complete as the Germans wanted. Their objective had been to destroy the Russian army "for all time." And though the Russians were demoralized, their army still existed.

One effect of this Russian defeat was the resignation of the Grand Duke as head of the Russian forces. He was replaced by the Czar, who was completely inept at military leadership.

Austrian troops pass through a Polish village as they pursue the Russian army. Here they are buying supplies from some of the villagers.

LIFE IN THE TRENCHES

The trenches along the western front were at first only shallow ditches. No one realized the trenches would be home for many soldiers for the next four years.

As the war dragged on, trenches were dug deep enough so that a man could walk through them without showing his head above ground. Tunnels and dugout rooms were hollowed out and reinforced to make sleeping and eating quarters. The trenches were often connected to the supply lines by a system of tunnels.

Belgian soldiers get haircuts from the trench barber. Close-cropped hair was important because body lice, or "cooties," would nest in body hair.

Left: shellfire all but destroyed a tree that stands at the end of this French soldier's trench. The only protection the men had against shell attacks was from their helmets and the sandbags piled above them. At the Second Battle of Ypres, the German artillery barrage went on for three days before the gas attack began. Below: an exploding shell lights up the night sky behind a British soldier. The trenches offered some protection against flying pieces of shrapnel from such explosions. Shelling often went on all night.

Left: Men in the trenches were often poorly supplied. Here are some ovens made from oil drums by British soldiers. Below: four British soldiers playing cards on a pile of trench mortar shells. In between attacks, a great danger was boredom. When morale dropped, the men failed to be on guard against the next attack.

These German soldiers seem relaxed in their trench home.

Defenses for the trenches became stronger as time went on. Many were reinforced with wood or concrete. The area between the two opposing sides was protected with barbed wire and land mines.

The trenches were very uncomfortable to live in. When it rained, men walked in mud up to their knees. The dampness and bad weather brought on pneumonia, influenza, and fungus skin diseases. The men were constantly bothered by rats and body lice. Days and nights were filled with the firing of artillery guns. Artillery attacks went on for days without stopping. Many men became "shell-shocked" from the continual fear and noise.

Most horrible of all was the order to go "over the top" and attack the other side. This was a virtual death sentence. The elaborate defenses made a successful attack impossible. Machine-gun fire raked the bodies of soldiers caught in the tangled barbed wire of "no-man's-land."

British soldiers in a dugout shelter during the Gallipoli campaign. In November, rain fell for an entire day on the men in the trenches, followed by sleet and then a snowstorm that left two feet of snow. Hundreds of soldiers on both sides drowned in the trenches. Many British soldiers froze to death as well, for lack of warm clothing.

The Austrian Alpenkorps was made up of skilled mountain fighters.

THE WAR BECOMES WORLDWIDE

New countries entered the war in 1915. In May, Italy declared war on Austria-Hungary, its old ally. Italy had been promised Austro-Hungarian territory by the Allies.

The Italians attacked the Austrians at the Isonzo River on the eastern border of Italy. This attack was launched over and over. Eleven battles of the Isonzo were fought during the war, and the Italians lost every one. Four such battles were fought in 1915, with the Italians losing 280,000 men.

Bulgaria entered the war on the side of the Central Powers in September, 1915. For its help, the Central Powers promised Bulgaria a part of Serbia called Macedonia. The Bulgarians, with German and Austrian help, crushed the Serbians. In October, Belgrade, the capital of Serbia, fell to the Central Powers.

The year 1915 also saw fighting in the German African colonies. The British, French, and Belgians used Africans from their colonies to defeat the Germans in the Cameroons, German Southwest Africa, and German East Africa.

There was fighting in the Near East as well. Britain, concerned about the Suez Canal, landed soldiers in Egypt and moved up through the Sinai Desert, meeting heavy resistance from Turkish soldiers.

Japan had entered the war in 1914 on the Allied side to occupy parts of China that had been under the influence of Germany. In 1915 Japan made 21 demands on China for additional territory. If China had agreed to all of them, it would have become a colony of Japan. China resisted but lost territory to the Japanese.

The war had now expanded far beyond Europe to become truly a world war.

A native village in the Cameroons becomes a victim of the war. Troops fighting against Germany are burning it.

THE STRUGGLE FOR THE SEAS

When war broke out, the British tried to score a quick victory over the German navy. But the Germans wanted to save the ships they had, and avoided contact with the British.

Only a few minor sea battles were fought in the early stages of the war. The German ship *Emden* raided Allied merchant ships in the Indian Ocean but was finally sunk on November 9, 1914.

The only German sea force of great size not safely in port was commanded by Admiral von Spee. His ships were off the coast of China when the war began. Von Spee set off across the Pacific. Near Chile he met a small British force and destroyed two British cruisers. The British were alarmed, and sent thirty ships after the five small ships of von Spee. Four of the German ships were sunk.

By early 1915 it was clear that the German navy could not compete with the British. The British had thrown a blockade around Germany, keeping ships from entering or leaving German ports. At first the British stopped only ships carrying war matériel. Soon, however, the British stopped any ship bound for Germany, including ships of neutral nations.

Part of the German fleet
sailing through the North Sea.

Night firing by a British gun-
boat. These ships were used as
artillery to stand offshore and
bombard an enemy port. They
could also clear the beaches to
prepare for a troop landing.

A convoy of British ships in
the North Sea at night. The
airplane escort was sometimes
able to spot approaching sub-
marines. Traveling in groups,
or convoys, merchant ships
could more easily be protected.

Some passengers rescued from the Lusitania.

To break the British blockade, the Germans turned to a new type of boat — the submarine. Called "U-boats" (for "Undersea boats"), they were very effective at sinking British warships. There was no way to warn the above-sea ships in advance or to save the crew of a sunken ship. Like the British, the Germans saw no difference between merchant ships carrying war matériel and warships.

A tragedy was sure to occur. The passenger ship *Lusitania* set sail from New York to England on May 1. The German embassy had taken an ad in the New York newspapers warning passengers not to sail on it. But only one passenger canceled. On May 7, off the coast of Ireland, the *Lusitania* was torpedoed by a U-boat. It sank, causing the deaths of almost 2,000 passengers, including 128 Americans.

The *Lusitania* incident was a costly mistake for the Germans. The attack angered citizens of the United States. Many Americans now favored entering the war on the Allied side.

The Battle of Jutland

In May and June of 1916 the British and German fleets finally met. The Germans planned to trap a small part of the British fleet in the North Sea. The British, however, had captured German codebooks and knew about this plan. They sent a large fleet to surprise and trap the Germans. But the British commander was able to escape by sacrificing some ships to save the fleet.

When the battle of Jutland was over, both sides claimed victory. The Germans actually sank more ships, and German naval weapons had been superior. Yet the British maintained control of the seas.

This picture shows a German shell falling near a British cruiser at the Battle of Jutland. Much of the smoke was caused by the coal-burning engines of the ships, not by exploding shells.

ACTION IN THE WEST

The Battle of Verdun

During the winter of 1915–16, General Falkenhayn, the German chief of staff, made plans for an offensive against the French. Falkenhayn picked a spot open to artillery attack yet necessary for the French to defend. His plan was to inflict such heavy casualties that the spirit of the French people would be broken.

The main objective of the attack was the line of French forts on the German border. The principal fort was at Verdun. The Germans began the attack on February 21 with the heaviest bombardment yet. Over a million artillery shells were fired against a 15-mile-wide front.

French troops pass through the ruins of Verdun. To the Germans, the amazing thing was that any troops had lived through the bombardment.

A French medical orderly bandages a wounded soldier.

The French sent General Pétain to organize the troops. The slogan of the French became "They shall not pass." Pétain moved to protect the single road that was his line of supply. Convoys of trucks and wagons rushed food, ammunition, and fresh troops along the "Sacred Way."

On February 25 the French fort at Douaumont fell to the Germans. Fighting shifted to Fort Vaux, which fell in June. Still the French held grimly on to Verdun.

Attacks by the Russians in the east and the beginning of the Allied offensive at the Somme diverted German troops away from Verdun. The fighting continued on a lesser scale all year until the French retook the forts at Douaumont and Vaux in October and November.

The Germans succeeded in draining the French of soldiers. But the Germans lost heavily too. By the end of the summer of 1916 the French had 315,000 casualties. The Germans had 281,000 casualties during the same period.

Results of the shelling at the Somme battlefield. Despite the devastation, the German trenches suffered relatively little damage. Some German trenches were dug as deep as 40 feet and were heavily reinforced.

The Battle of the Somme

Because of Verdun, the British had to assume the biggest part in the Battle of the Somme, the bloodiest battle of the war. Originally, the British commander, Douglas Haig, agreed that if the casualties at the Somme were too great he would stop the offensive. He did not keep his word.

After five days and nights of heavy bombardment against an 18-mile front, the British and French went over the top on July 1. The Allies thought there would be nothing left of the enemy defenses but a hole in the ground. Instead, the craters caused by the shelling made it difficult for the attacking soldiers to run. The soldiers were each carrying 66 pounds of equipment as well. On the first day, 60,000 British soldiers were cut down by machine-gun fire in no-man's-land. Still Haig refused to break off the attack. The fighting went on till November.

In the Battle of the Somme, the British had 420,000 casualties. The French casualties were 204,000, and the German about 500,000. General Haig was promoted to field marshal for his work.

The most important event of the battle was the introduction of the tank. This weapon would change modern warfare. It gave the offensive side mobility and protection. At the Somme, however, the tanks were used ineffectively. Too few of them were available. Ironically, the Battle of the Somme was the last time cavalry troops were used in a major military battle.

Left: an 8-inch howitzer firing during the artillery barrage at the Somme. A million and a half shells were fired on the German lines in the first six days of the Allied attack. Below: one of the casualties at the Battle of Somme. The final total was over 1 million. The constant fire devastated the area.

ACTION IN THE EAST

The Brusilov Offensive

In early 1916 the Allies again asked Russia to open a campaign to draw German troops away from the western front. Russia was eager to regain the territory it had lost in 1915. On JUNE 4 the Russian general Brusilov attacked the Austro-Hungarian front. In three days the Russian army took 200,000 Austrian prisoners. The morale of the Austro-Hungarian army reached a low point from which it never recovered.

Unfortunately, General Brusilov needed reserve troops to follow up the victory. Brusilov's men were south of the needed reserves, and the railroads in the area ran only east to west.

Brusilov decided to advance without the reserve troops. He ran into Austrians reinforced by German soldiers who had been intended for Verdun. After heavy fighting and great losses of men, Brusilov retreated.

Rumania had been impressed by the first successes of the Brusilov offensive and entered the war on the side of the Allies. This was a costly mistake. Rumania had a large supply of oil and grain. The Germans quickly overran Rumania and seized the supplies, which were useful in continuing the war.

Russian soldiers preparing for attack.

The French brought soldiers into the war from their colonies all over the world. These soldiers, landing at Salonika, are Annamites from Cochin China. Cochin China was part of what today is Vietnam.

Since there was not enough room for all the soldiers coming into Salonika, many of them had to go out into the countryside nearby. These two British officers are discussing "billets," or living quarters, with a Greek countrywoman.

Salonika

Allied troops first landed at Salonika, Greece, in 1915 to help Serbia defend itself against attack. After Serbia was occupied, the Serbian troops retired to Salonika. In 1916 the Allies landed more troops there to attack the Central Powers in the Balkans. They were unsuccessful, but a permanent base was established at Salonika. The Allies continued to put pressure on the Central Powers from this spot for the remainder of the war.

THE NEW WEAPONS OF WAR

When it became apparent that the war would last longer than expected, the search began for a super-weapon that would quickly bring a dramatic victory. Instead of shortening the war, however, the new weapons only increased the cost of it, both in money and in human lives.

Both sides designed and built huge artillery guns for the days-long barrages that came before each attack. The most extreme example of the great guns was the "Paris gun," which the Germans used to attack Paris. It could fire a cannon shell 82 miles. The Germans brought the gun by railroad to a forest 75 miles from Paris. When the shells began landing in the city, no one could imagine where they were coming from, since the sound of the gun firing could not be heard that far away. Even so, the gun was not a success. It took 15 minutes to load. Its barrel had to be replaced after firing only 60 shots. Finally, the gun could not be aimed accurately.

A drawing of the "Paris gun." The barrel was so heavy that it had to be supported from overhead.

Because it didn't live up to expectations, it was taken back to Germany. It was never found after the war.

More and more poison gases were developed by both sides. Many affected the eyes and skin as well as the lungs and throat. Different types of gas masks were produced to counter the effect of the gases. Sometimes changing winds blew the gas back against the soldiers who had released it.

At first there was no way to direct gas attacks toward enemy troops unless the wind was blowing in the right direction, as shown above. Later, cannons were used to fire containers of gas. Gas masks used early in the war were rags or pieces of cotton dipped in water or chemicals and tied to the face. Later, more effective gas masks were developed. Masks were also provided for horses, mules, and guard dogs.

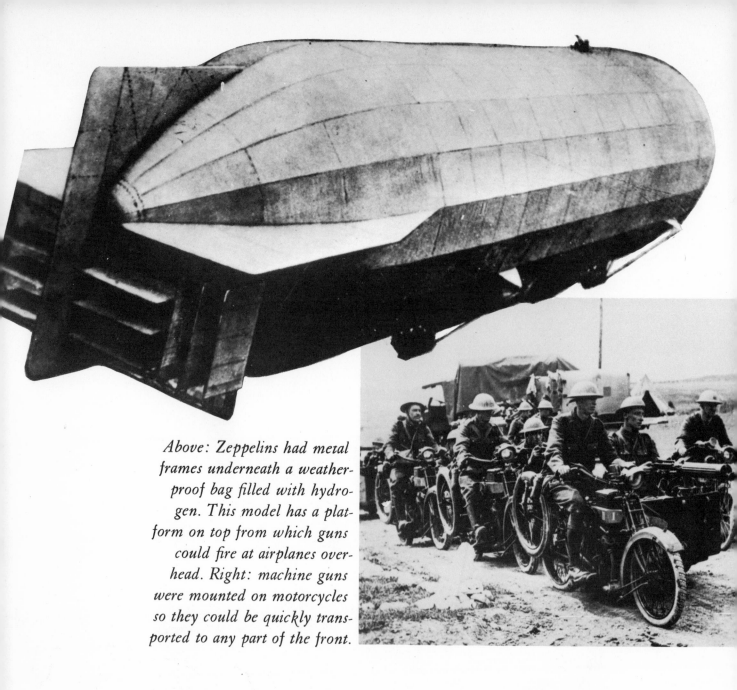

Above: Zeppelins had metal frames underneath a weather-proof bag filled with hydrogen. This model has a platform on top from which guns could fire at airplanes overhead. Right: machine guns were mounted on motorcycles so they could be quickly transported to any part of the front.

Zeppelins and airplanes were first used for military purposes in World War I. At the beginning of the war, both the airplane and the Zeppelin were used for scouting enemy positions. Later in the war, some were used for bombing missions, but the slow airplane and even slower Zeppelin were easily shot down.

Hand-cranked machine guns had been used since the nineteenth century, but now technology produced gas-propelled guns that could shoot many rounds of ammunition quickly. Mass cavalry charges fell easily before a squad of machine gunners, and cavalry became obsolete.

Modern transportation was important to winning the war. In 1914 soldiers and equipment were transported by horses and wagons. By the war's end, motor vehicles and trains were the chief means of supply and troop movement. Countries without an extensive railway system, such as Russia and the Ottoman Empire, were at a great disadvantage.

The super-weapon that both sides were looking for was actually built, although its importance was not recognized until later. This was the tank. Tanks easily broke through the enemy lines, even crossing the no-man's-land with ease. None of the generals seemed at first to realize that a massed attack of troops following the tanks could break the enemy line for good. Not until World War II were tanks generally used with troop movements.

The tank was not affected by gas or rifle fire. Only a direct hit by a cannon could stop it.

Durch unser Heer · das freie Meer!

WOMEN OF BRITAIN SAY – "GO!"

The Germans, like all the participants in the war, saw themselves as fighting for a just cause. This poster shows a German soldier as a defender of freedom of the seas.

It had been the British tradition to use volunteers in the army. This poster was typical of the campaign of volunteer enlistment. In 1916, for the first time, the British drafted soldiers.

STALEMATE AT THE END OF 1916

From the beginning of the war, both sides made use of propaganda. The British and French called the Germans "Huns" and said they must be defeated to save civilization. The Germans portrayed themselves nobly, as fighters for freedom and the glory of Germany. Patriotic songs, posters, and pamphlets were all part of the propaganda effort.

But the reality and ugliness of the war were felt at home. Casualty lists were printed in the newspapers — thousands of names long. Young men had gone off to war full of enthusiasm and bravery and now they were never coming back.

People at home saw that little ground was being gained by either side. The leaders had said the war would be short. Now two years had gone by and there seemed to be no end in sight.

In Germany the Allied shipping blockade was having a serious effect. Food was getting scarce, even in Berlin. It was hard to keep the troops adequately supplied. Hindenburg and Ludendorff replaced Falkenhayn at the end of August. Symbolized by the monogram HL, they increased their power over the government as well as the army.

In Austria-Hungary, Emperor Franz Joseph, who had reigned since 1848, died. His grand-nephew replaced him on the throne and dismissed the generals who had done so poorly.

The Easter Rebellion of 1916 in Ireland temporarily diverted British attention from the war. Money and soldiers had to be used to put down the Irish rebels. David Lloyd George became the new prime minister of Britain. In France, General Nivelle replaced Joffre as commander in chief.

But the greatest changes were to come in Russia. In 1917 there would be a revolution. Along with the entrance of the United States into the war, this would bring an end to the stalemate of 1916.

One of a series of French drawings accusing the Germans of atrocities. Germans claimed similar atrocities by the British and French.

THE RUSSIAN REVOLUTION

Discontent among the Russian soldiers and people had been building for a long time. Soldiers went into battle without proper equipment or training. At home, a corrupt and inefficient government ruled over a country that was hungry and poor. The Czar's leadership of the army showed him to be weak and inept.

While these Russian soldiers were equipped with rifles, many were sent to the front with only bayonets tied to sticks.

A scene from the Russian revolution.
Bullets are being fired from the
public library. Some people are running
to seek shelter, while others lie
dead and wounded in the street.

The February Revolution

In late February of 1917, riots broke out in St. Petersburg, the capital of Russia. On March 11 the Czar called troops to put down the rebellion. But the soldiers joined the rebellion.

Violence spread throughout the country. The Czar was forced to resign. A new government, under the leadership of Alexander Kerensky, took over. Workers and soldiers organized committees known as "soviets" and agreed to cooperate with Kerensky's government.

Now Kerensky made a fatal mistake. The people of Russia wanted peace, food, and land. But Kerensky, under pressure from the Allies, decided to continue the war.

Russian and Austrian soldiers fraternizing at the front in 1917.

The Russian Offensive

The Russian army, commanded by General Brusilov, attacked the Austrians in the area of the Carpathians. On July 5 the Russians crushed the Austrian and German forces and gained 20 miles. But then the Russian army quit. The soldiers refused to go forward. The Austrians and Germans counterattacked and regained all the lost ground. Brusilov was replaced by General Kornilov, but to no avail. The soldiers would not fight.

The Bolshevik Revolution

Meanwhile, Ludendorff arranged for a train to take a Russian revolutionary named Nikolai Lenin from Switzerland through Germany and Finland to Russia. Ludendorff wanted Russia out of the war for good, and Lenin had said he would stop the fighting if he was in power. Lenin was the leader of a group called the Bolsheviks. They not only wanted to get out of the war but also promised "all power to the workers." Today they are called Communists.

In November, 1917, the soviet and the army units in the capital withdrew their support from Kerensky. Lenin, now certain of support from the army, ordered a revolt. On November 7 the Bolsheviks seized control of the country. The next day, Lenin issued a peace decree, taking Russia out of the war.

The Treaty of Brest-Litovsk

Peace negotiations between Germany and the Bolshevik government began in December, 1917, in the town of Brest-Litovsk. The talks were broken off when the Germans demanded large parts of Russian territory. In January Leon Trotsky began negotiations for the Russians again. Trotsky said Russia would leave the war without signing a formal treaty. The Germans then attacked and took the entire Ukraine, a great farming area of Russia. Finally the Russians signed the Treaty of Brest-Litovsk on March 3, 1918.

In the treaty Russia lost a third of its population, a third of its farmland, and about half of its industry. Germany's harshness toward Russia was a warning to the other Allies of what they could expect if they lost the war to Germany.

Above: **Nikolai Lenin.**
Left: Russian prisoners playing cards.

A dead soldier, unburied for many months. Sights like this were common during the war.

ACTION IN THE WEST

The Nivelle Offensive

When General Robert Nivelle took command of the French army from General Joffre in December, 1916, he said he had a plan to break the German line. Actually the plan was no different from previous ones, except that it would be launched without an artillery barrage beforehand.

But the Germans found out where Nivelle's attack was to take place. They pulled out of the area and took up positions in the strongly defended rear position known as the Hindenburg Line. Even so, Nivelle went ahead with the offensive on April 16. The result was a great French defeat and the loss of many lives. This was the last straw for the French army. Many of the soldiers put down their arms and refused to fight.

Mutiny

The mutiny of the French troops lasted for two months. The French kept news of the mutiny from the Germans, and there were no German attacks during this time.

General Pétain was put in charge of the French army. His position was delicate. The mutiny called for discipline, but punishment might cause the mutiny to spread. Pétain visited the soldiers at the front. They were angry because they were being slaughtered for no apparent purpose. Pétain saw that the soldiers needed a regular system of leaves (vacations), to recover from the hardships of the trenches. Eventually, he restored morale and discipline. The new motto of the French army was "Lavish with steel, stingy with blood."

The Battle of Passchendaele

General Haig persuaded Lloyd George to allow him to launch still another British attack, in the area of Ypres. For two years the British had been digging under the German positions and mining them with tons of explosives. On June 7 the explosives were set off. About 20,000 German soldiers were killed or wounded.

The British soldiers pressed forward and took many prisoners. But the Germans recovered and regrouped. The battle went on through a rainy summer that turned the land into a swamp. Finally, winter ended the battle. The British had gained 1,000 yards of territory at the cost of 300,000 British soldiers.

Machine gunners in action, wearing their gas helmets. Since the newly developed mustard gas burned the skin, the helmet had to cover the entire head.

The Battle of Cambrai

The only bright spot for the Allies in 1917 was the Battle of Cambrai, fought in November. Two British generals organized an attack, using 324 of the new tanks. Their objective was the French town of Cambrai, which was surrounded by solid dry ground that could support the attacking tanks. Using a smoke screen, the British successfully penetrated more than 5 miles on the first day, losing only 4,000 casualties. This was more territory than had been won the previous four months at Ypres. Haig did not follow up the victory, however. He needed the soldiers to support Caporetto.

Below: a British soldier showing the helmet that saved his life. Left: a British sign near Ypres shows the grim humor of the war.

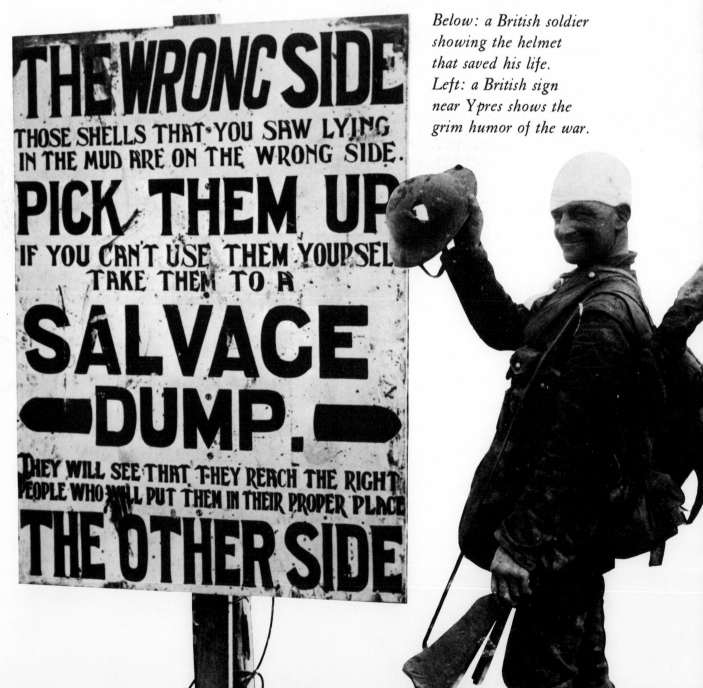

An Italian motorcycle squad. Part of the problem with the Italian army was its commander, whose motto was "The leader is always right, especially when he is wrong."

Italian prisoners with their Austrian captors. At Caporetto, thousands of Italians deserted. They were said to have run to the Austrian side shouting, "Long live Austria!" and "On to Rome!"

The Battle of Caporetto

Bad news arrived from Italy. After the many futile Italian attacks at the Isonzo River, Austria decided to crush the Italian army once and for all. With German help, the Austrians attacked at Caporetto on October 24 and destroyed more than one fourth of the Italian army. The rest of the Italians fled in disorder. The British and French had to rush troops to support Italy. Ultimately the Austrian and German advance was stopped by bad weather.

(65)

ACTION IN THE NEAR EAST

Mesopotamia and Palestine

The year 1917 was decisive in the fighting in the Near East. There were two major British victories.

The British had invaded Mesopotamia in 1915 with a force from India. Meeting little resistance at first, they got as far as the town of Kut-el-Amara, Iraq. Their objective was Baghdad, the capital city. But the desert heat and superior numbers of Turkish soldiers gradually stopped the British offensive. Through the year 1916 the campaign see-sawed back and forth. At last, in March, 1917, Baghdad finally fell to the British forces.

In 1915 the British had landed in Egypt to protect the Suez Canal from the Turks. The British forces advanced to the city of Gaza, where they were stopped until 1917. The terrain was difficult and the weather scorching.

Czechoslovakian legionnaires posing before a pyramid and the Sphinx. They fought on the side of the British in the Egyptian and Mesopotamian desert campaigns.

British infantry during the Mesopotamian campaign. The temperature in the desert could rise as high as 140 degrees for an entire day.

In early 1917 General Allenby was appointed to head the Palestine campaign. Lloyd George asked him to take Jerusalem "as a Christmas present for the British people." First the British captured the wells at Beersheba, in order to have a water supply for the campaign. In November, Allenby's forces took Gaza at last, and headed up toward Jerusalem. They were aided by Arabs led by a young British officer named T. E. Lawrence, later known as Lawrence of Arabia. Allenby took Jerusalem in December, giving the British people their present.

Russia vs. Turkey
In 1916 the Russians captured most of the Turkish province of Armenia. They found there the results of the most ghastly event of the war. The Turks had expected the Armenians to try to gain their independence by allying with the invading Russians. So the Turks ordered a massacre of the entire Armenian population. At least a million men, women, and children were killed.

American soldiers arriving in France show their enthusiasm.

AMERICA ENTERS THE WAR

Reasons for Entry

A majority of Americans had long been sympathetic to the Allies. The sinking of the *Lusitania* in 1915 had angered many citizens. Also, the United States had been making loans to the Allied side. If the Allies lost, these loans would not be repaid. Finally, some Americans felt that German domination of Europe would be against American interests.

But many Americans of German and Irish descent were opposed to the Allies. President Wilson had asked all Americans to be neutral in thought as well as in deed.

Then, early in 1917, the Germans announced they were resuming unrestricted submarine warfare. The United States broke off relations with the German government in protest. Another provocation to the United States was the Zimmermann Telegram. The Zimmermann

Telegram was sent in January, 1917, from the German Foreign Office to the German ambassador in Mexico. The British intercepted and decoded it. The telegram told the German ambassador to offer Texas, New Mexico, and Arizona to Mexico. In return Mexico was to help attack the United States in case of war.

On March 16, 1917, U-boats torpedoed two American ships. On the same day, the Kerensky government came to power in Russia. Most Americans felt the new Russian government was democratic and deserved support against the Germans.

On April 5, 1917, the United States declared war on the Central Powers. Its great industrial strength was ready to help the Allies.

*These men decided to resume unrestricted submarine warfare —
Kaiser **Wilhelm** (center), General **von Hindenburg** (left), and
General **Ludendorff** (right). Because the Kaiser's left arm
was withered from childhood polio, it was the custom for
others to conceal one arm when in his presence.*

The Yanks Are Coming

When the United States declared war, its army and navy were small. A law was passed to draft young men, and training camps were set up.

The country united behind the war effort. Women moved into jobs left by men. Children collected material that could be used for making war equipment. Thousands of tin cans were rescued from the garbage, stamped flat, and tied into bundles. Great mounds of peach pits were collected to be used in making filters for gas masks. Victory gardens were planted in backyards across America. Everyone took part in helping win the war.

A small force of American soldiers was sent to Europe in 1917, mainly to give a lift to Allied morale. General John Pershing ("Black Jack") was its commander.

American infantrymen in France, practicing bayonet thrusts. Infantrymen were called "doughboys." One explanation for the term dates to Pershing's army in Texas. The troops on horseback called the infantrymen "adobes" because the dust powdered their uniforms. "Adobes" was shortened to "dobies" and later changed to "doughboys."

*A French couple greets
two American soldiers.*

The American Expeditionary Force marched into Paris on July 4. Crowds cheered. Hope arose throughout the Allied countries that the tide of war would now turn.

The Americans saw their first action in October. They were sent to a quiet section of the front near the Swiss border. On November 3 a German company on the opposite side opened an attack. They expected the Americans to flee. But the "doughboys" fought bravely. The Germans were thrown back. The Americans lost eleven prisoners and three dead. Now they were in the war.

THE FOURTEEN POINTS

On January 8, 1918, President Wilson announced a plan for a lasting peace. He called his proposals the Fourteen Points. The points were:

1. The end of secret treaties.
2. Freedom of the seas.
3. The end of economic trade barriers between countries.
4. Reducing the military arms races.
5. Giving rights to colonial peoples.
6. Return of Russian territory and allowing Russia freely to choose its own government.
7. Return of Belgian territory.
8. Return of Alsace-Lorraine to France.
9. Adjusting the border of Italy fairly.
10. Allowing the peoples within the Austro-Hungarian Empire to form their own countries.
11. Return of Rumanian, Serbian, and Montenegrin territory and granting Serbia access to the sea.
12. Opening the Dardanelles Strait and allowing non-Turks within the Ottoman Empire to form their own countries.
13. Allowing Poland to become an independent nation and giving it access to the sea.
14. Formation of a world group of nations to preserve world peace. (This was to become the League of Nations.)

All of Wilson's points seemed good for the world. People in all countries, including the Central Powers, were impressed. But the leaders of nations who had been fighting since 1914 felt they should receive territory if they won the war. The greediness of the politicians cast a shadow over the Fourteen Points.

Right: two German soldiers with carrier pigeons. Carrier pigeons were useful for sending messages because they could not be intercepted.

Left: an ambulance driver poses with a young French admirer. One of the reforms Pétain carried out in the French army was to improve the quality of the medical service.

Those too young
and too old
to fight stayed
at home to do
their part by
producing food
for the soldiers.

A female bus conductor collecting
fares from two servicemen in London.
Before the war, such a job was con-
sidered "improper" for a woman.

THE HOME FRONT

As the casualty lists grew, it seemed as if the side "with the last 100,000 men to throw into battle" would win. On the "home front," governments had to convince the people that the sacrifice of men was worthwhile. All the countries had to draft men to continue the war.

The men who went to war had to be replaced at home in the factories and on the farms. Women began taking these jobs. Many were never again content to be restricted to housework. Their new attitudes would bring social changes after the war.

The home front was also a struggle to produce enough military goods. Steel, copper, and tin had to be reserved for military uses. Germany was particularly short of raw materials because of the British blockade. Walther Rathenau was appointed to take charge of all the factories in Germany. Rathenau and his staff told each company what goods to make and where to get the materials. German workers were told where to work, and were not allowed to leave. Laborers were brought in from occupied territories to help the German war effort.

The money spent on running the war was staggering. Most European countries had to borrow heavily, particularly from the United States. Governments took over greater economic power, and government planning continued after the war.

These boys from Cooperstown, New York, knitted socks and sweaters for men in the army.

WAR IN THE AIR

The airplane was still a new invention in 1914. Neither side expected it to have any great effect on the war. Its chief use was to scout and spy on enemy troop movements and gun placements. Even for these limited uses, the airplane was not as good as a balloon or a Zeppelin.

In the beginning of the war, a pilot's life was usually not in danger. Enemy pilots usually waved at each other. As the war went on, pilots began carrying pistols and rifles and firing at each other. Machine guns were mounted on planes, but they could shoot only off to the sides. A pilot attempting to shoot in the direction he was flying often shot off his own propeller. Then a Dutch scientist named Fokker, who worked for the Germans, invented a way to synchronize a machine gun with a propeller. For a while the Fokker planes ruled the skies. Then the British captured one of the Fokkers and developed their own fighter planes.

A French pilot checks the sight on his gun before taking off. This plane was a biplane, having two wings. The faster Fokker planes had only one wing, making them easier to maneuver.

Above: most World War I planes were single-seaters. The pilot was his own gunner, navigator, bombardier, and, on occasion, photographer. Aerial photographs were often a great help to forces on the ground. Left: the method of taking aerial pictures was quite simple. Although bulky by today's standards, the cameras were lighter than most models of the time.

The war in the air captured the imagination of people at home. Even troops in the trenches cheered as they watched a "dogfight" going on overhead. The propaganda machines helped to glamorize the fighting pilots. A pilot who shot down 5 enemy planes was known as an ace. The famous Red Baron of Germany, Baron von Richthofen, shot down 80 Allied planes before he was killed by a Canadian pilot. The Allied ace of aces was a Frenchman, René Fonck, who had 75 "kills." The British ace Edward Mannock had 73 "kills" even though he was blind in one eye. The champion American ace was Eddie Rickenbacker, who shot down 26 enemy planes.

In January, 1915, a new kind of air war began. German Zeppelins bombed British towns and cities. On May 31 London itself was bombed. Over the next 18 months, 557 British citizens were killed and 1,360 injured in bombing attacks by Zeppelins.

The Germans hoped that the British would be terrified by the Zeppelin attacks, but the citizens remained calm. The Germans lost many Zeppelins from ground fire and British airplane attacks. Filled with flammable gas, the Zeppelins exploded if their skin was pierced by a bomb or incendiary bullet.

In June, 1917, German Gotha planes bombed London in a raid that killed or wounded nearly 600 people. In the remaining months of the war, the British developed their own bomber plane.

Although none of the bombing raids was crucial in the war, each changed warfare for the future. Soldiers and sailors were no longer the only ones whose lives were in danger. In modern war, people living in cities far from the action were exposed to death from the sky. The home front in the future would be as dangerous as the battle front.

Opposite, right: German pilot modeling an "aviator's suit." Because the pilot's compartment was cold and windy, the suit was completely heated. Left: the mechanism for dropping bombs was often very crude. Some pilots carried bombs inside their compartments and threw them over the side. The bomb shown here is a typical size.

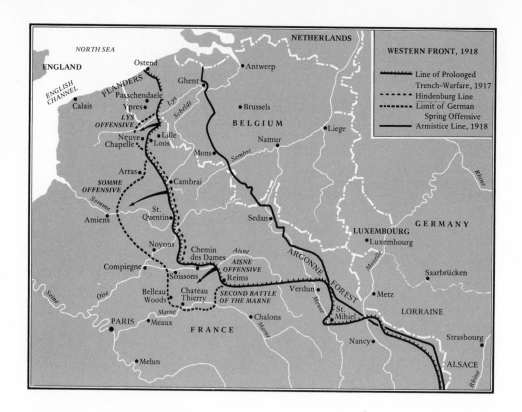

WAR IN THE WEST

Germany Gambles All

At the beginning of 1918 the Germans were becoming desperate. The British blockade was more effective than ever. The Germans were running out of supplies. The Americans were in the war. But Ludendorff knew he had a few months before the United States could mobilize and send troops. Also, Russia being out of the war allowed him to transfer soldiers to the western front.

In this situation, Ludendorff decided to gamble on total victory in the spring of 1918. With one great attack, Germany might defeat Britain and France before the Americans could arrive in force.

The Germans picked the weakest spots in the Allied lines for the assault. The first attacks were in Artois and Picardy. This part of the front was defended by British forces. Ludendorff hoped to drive the British back to the English Channel.

The battle began on March 21, near Amiens. A thick fog helped the German forces advance without warning. The British line was broken on the first day, and the Germans made greater gains in the next few days. The British began to retreat.

The British and French held a war council. The British were determined to hold the line and the German soldiers were too exhausted to pursue farther. The offensive stopped on April 5. The Germans had gained 1,250 square miles of desolated French countryside. The objective of driving the British to the sea, however, had failed.

The Battle of the Lys

Ludendorff turned to the area of Ypres once again. In an offensive called the Battle of the Lys, he made another attempt to crush the British forces. The offensive began April 9 with another huge bombardment and gained 5 miles the first day. The Germans pressed forward, but at a slower pace, over the next several days. An officer back from the front told Ludendorff the men were too busy searching for food to move any faster.

The Germans breaking through British lines in March, 1918. Ludendorff counted on using the same tactics that had worked for him in Russia. "We chop a hole. The rest follow," he explained. What went wrong was that the British and French reinforced holes in the line quicker than the Russians had been able to.

Although the British had lost ground, their defensive line was now drawn together, giving them a superior position. On April 25, the Germans tried to advance again, but the British, with supporting French troops, drove back the attack.

The Aisne Offensive

Now Ludendorff switched to the southern part of the western front. He chose the area north of the Aisne River on a ridge called Chemin des Dames. The Germans started their bombardment on May 27. They tore through the center of the Allied line, and swept forward, crossing the Aisne and then the Vesle River. By June 3 they reached the Marne River, east of the town of Château-Thierry. They were 37 miles from Paris. But the Americans were on the way.

The American Third Division rushed to the Marne. On the way they passed French soldiers who told them the war was over. But the Americans held the line at the Marne. A second battle between American and German troops took place west of Château-Thierry, with another American victory. The German offensive halted on June 6.

An American soldier, wearing the helmet of an officer of the Prussian Guard, posing in a shell hole.

An American
machine-gun
platoon from the
8th Division,
advancing
through a woods
in France
late in the war.

Americans firing
at a German
airplane. Anti-
aircraft guns
were used by
both sides but
were not very
effective.

Right: Germans defending a position in France. By late in 1918 even the German soldiers in the trenches realized the war was lost. Between August and October the Allies took almost 300,000 German prisoners. Below: British tanks. The smoke screen was often used in attacks to permit movement without detection by the enemy.

The Allied Counterattack

Now began an Allied counterattack. One of the decisive battles was at Belleau Wood, a hunting preserve west of Château-Thierry. The Germans prepared for a major defense. The American Second Division, probably the best American fighting unit, was selected to attack.

On June 6, the attack began. American marines occupied the southern section of Belleau Wood. Fierce fighting continued until the marines retreated to allow their artillery to destroy German positions. Soon more units arrived and Belleau Wood fell on June 25.

Belleau Wood was a great psychological victory for the Americans. The Germans, who had not believed the Americans would be effective fighters, now called them *Teufelhunden,* or "devil dogs."

Ludendorff ordered a fourth offensive south of Amiens, which failed after the Germans had penetrated 9 miles. Again Ludendorff ordered his forces to strike. This final effort came on July 15 against the French and is known as the Second Battle of the Marne.

The Second Battle of the Marne

This time the French were better prepared. The Germans penetrated their line, but the French counterattacked on July 18, using tanks. The German front broke. The battle continued for three days. At its end the Germans were in full retreat. Ludendorff's gamble had failed.

Along the Somme, the British, Canadians, and Australians launched a major attack at Amiens on August 8. The attack was planned to make effective use of tanks. There was no artillery barrage beforehand. Instead, the tanks led the attack, with the infantry following close behind. In less than two hours the British captured 15,000 prisoners and 400 German artillery pieces. Ludendorff later wrote: "August 8 was the black day of the German army."

The last big German salient lay south of Verdun at the town of Saint-Mihiel. American colonel Billy Mitchell led 1,500 Allied planes in bombing this position. On September 12 American ground troops attacked and the bulge collapsed. Now the counteroffensive of the Allies was launched all along the line. The stalemate was over, and defeat for Germany was only a matter of time.

VICTORY IN THE EAST

The war was going badly for the Central Powers on all fronts. In the Near East the British troops followed up their victory in Jerusalem by taking the Syrian city of Damascus. The Ottoman Empire surrendered on October 30.

The Allied soldiers who had been bottled up in Salonika broke out. They routed the Bulgarian army and forced Bulgaria to sign a truce on September 29.

The last Austrian offensive was stopped on the Piave River in June. The Italians counterattacked across the Piave and defeated Austria's forces in late October. Austria-Hungary asked for an armistice on November 3.

VICTORY IN THE WEST

The Allied counteroffensive in the west continued. The British broke through the Hindenburg Line at the end of September. October saw a successful Allied offensive in Flanders. The final Allied drive was the Meuse-Argonne offensive, during which many Americans lost their lives in the Argonne Forest.

Germany was falling apart. The Kaiser forced Ludendorff to resign, and the German navy mutinied. Finally Hindenburg advised the Kaiser to abdicate, and Germany surrendered.

ARMISTICE

On November 11 the armistice was signed. The Germans surrendered on the basis of Wilson's Fourteen Points.

The armistice was greeted with joy all over the world. The soldiers at the front broke into cheers. They ran across the barren and wasted no-man's-land. In the midst of the destruction there was a feeling of joy. The war was over!

The armistice
celebration
as it looked
in London's
Fleet Street.

MIL
RUBBE
HEEL
& TIP

OD
NE
RES

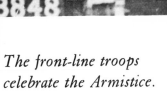

The front-line troops
celebrate the Armistice.

The "Big Four."
Left to right:
Lloyd George,
Orlando,
Clemenceau,
and Wilson.

Germany's defeated
troops arrive in
Berlin. As the men
pass through the
Brandenburg Gate,
onlookers show
little enthusiasm.
Military leaders
such as Ludendorff
were later to claim
that the German
army was "stabbed
in the back" by
the politicians
who surrendered.

THE VERSAILLES CONFERENCE

With the war over, all eyes turned to President Wilson. His Fourteen Points had brought hope to millions. When Wilson arrived in Europe at the end of 1918, he was greeted as a hero.

The peace conference met at Versailles in late January. Most of the decisions were made by the "Big Four" — Orlando of Italy, Clemenceau of France, Lloyd George of Britain, and Wilson of the United States. Contrary to the traditions of European diplomacy, there were no representatives from the defeated countries. All of the winners except Wilson wanted to collect the spoils of war.

THE PEACE TREATY

The treaty that was finally written was a mixture of Wilson's idealism and the Allied nations' desire to collect spoils. A section of the treaty blamed the war entirely on the Central Powers, especially Germany. This section caused bitterness among the defeated nations. The victors demanded that the losers pay the costs of the war.

The treaty returned Alsace and Lorraine to France. Belgium was evacuated, and given a small strip of German territory. The country of Poland was established with territory taken from Russia, Austria-Hungary, and Germany. Czechoslovakia was created with territory from Austria-Hungary. Yugoslavia was created from Serbian and Montenegrin land, along with Austro-Hungarian land. Italy gained some territory. The German colonies in Africa and non-Turkish parts of the Ottoman Empire were entrusted to the Allies. These areas were to become independent later.

Wilson justified his compromises on the grounds that the League of Nations was the most important part of the treaty. The league would correct any wrongs written into the treaty. But the United States never joined the league, and the league never had the power that Wilson thought it should have.

THE EFFECTS OF THE WAR

World War I changed the lives of millions of people throughout the world. The society of prewar Europe was completely disrupted. The seeds were sown for another great war twenty years later.

Costs of the War

World War I was the most expensive war fought up to that time. In lives, the cost was about 8½ million soldiers dead and about 20 million wounded. Almost 18 million soldiers were taken prisoner or missing in action. Many civilians were killed, and disease and hunger brought on by the war took many more lives.

The cost of the war in dollars cannot be measured. Before the war, the countries of Europe were "creditor nations" — other countries owed them money. After 1918 they were "debtor nations" — they owed money to other countries. The United States became the world's strongest nation economically.

Crippled German soldiers with artificial limbs at work in a shop making bandages. One German soldier who bitterly resented defeat was a corporal named Adolf Hitler. In 1933 he would come to power in Germany. In 1939 his troops marched into Poland, starting World War II.

*Over and over, the battles of war raged around
the town of Ypres, Belgium. This is what remained
of the 700-year-old cathedral in the town.
The Germans shelled it because they said it was
being used as an observation post. To bury the
dead at Ypres, 140 cemeteries were needed.*

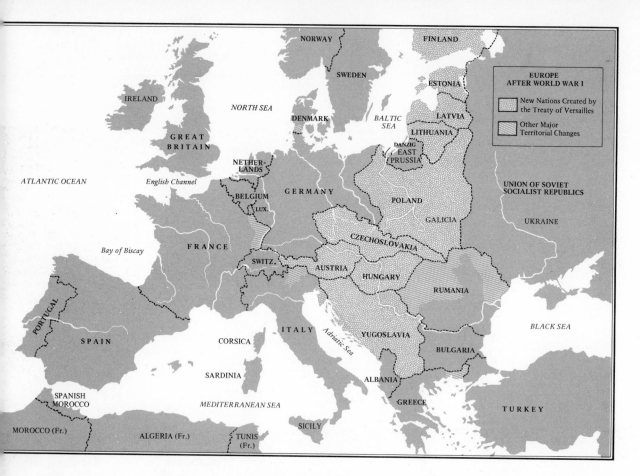

Map legend:

EUROPE
AFTER WORLD WAR I

☐ New Nations Created by the Treaty of Versailles
☐ Other Major Territorial Changes

Change in the Map of Europe

The war changed the map of Europe forever. Where the Austro-Hungarian Empire had been before, there were now two countries, Austria and Hungary, much reduced in size. The non-Austrian and non-Hungarian parts of the empire became parts of Poland, Czechoslovakia, and Yugoslavia.

Russia lost territory to Poland, Finland, and the new Baltic nations of Latvia, Estonia, and Lithuania. But most important was Russia's new status as a Communist country which changed the political life of Europe.

Loss of Confidence

The death of millions of young men wiped out a whole generation of possible leaders. Those who survived the war were often permanently scarred, either emotionally or physically. The air of confidence with which Europeans entered the war was changed to fear and uncertainty. And the war itself left bitterness that would lead to an even more terrible war.

(92)

*"The lamps are going out
all over Europe.
We will not see them
lit again in our time."*

Sir Edward Grey, 1914

INDEX

(94)